A Keepsake Book about
God & Me

To Vance, my grandson, for whom this book was written

by Rebecca A. Egbert
Illustrated by Nancy Woodman

Tyndale House Publishers, Inc.
WHEATON • ILLINOIS

God made me.

I am _____ years old.

My birthday is

_____

Just-for-fun

I will draw my birthday cake.

I will draw _____ candles on my cake.

My picture:

My name:

_____

_____

"Know that the Lord is God. It is he who made us, and we are his."

Psalm 100:3

I am special

God made me different
from everyone else.

Just-for-fun I will draw a picture of my face.

I will color my eyes

_____

I will color my hair

_____

I will color my face

_____

"I praise you because I am . . . wonderfully made."

Psalm 139:14

My baby picture

God knew me before I was born.

"Before I formed you in the womb I knew you."

Jeremiah 1:5

Just-for-fun
I will glue my baby picture here.

In this picture I am _____ old.

I was born on
☐ Sunday
☐ Monday
☐ Tuesday
☐ Wednesday
☐ Thursday
☐ Friday
☐ Saturday

at _____ o'clock

in the _____

My hands

God gave me hands.

Things I can do with my hands:

clap while I sing
☐ yes ☐ no

snap my fingers
☐ yes ☐ no

throw a ball
☐ yes ☐ no

tickle a friend
☐ yes ☐ no

make a sandwich
☐ yes ☐ no

play the piano
☐ yes ☐ no

walk upside down
☐ yes ☐ no

Just-for-fun I will draw around my hands.

This is my
right hand.

This is my
left hand.

"Clap your hands, all you nations; shout to God with cries of joy."

Psalm 47:1

My feet

God gave me feet so I can run and play.

Just-for-fun
I will draw
around my feet.

This is my left foot.

I wear size _____ shoes.

This is my
right foot.

"Your word is
a lamp to
my feet."

Psalm 119:105

God makes me grow.

Just-for-fun I will measure myself. I will use a tape measure or a ruler.

My head is _____ inches around.

My neck is _____ inches around.

"And Jesus grew in wisdom and stature, and in favor with God and men."

Luke 2:52

My arm is _____ inches around.

My mouth is _____ inches wide.

My leg is _____ inches around.

My waist is _____ inches around.

I am _____ feet _____ inches tall.
I weigh _____ pounds.

God gave me a family.

These are the people in my family:

_____

_____

_____

_____

_____

_____

_____

_____

_____

_____

_____

Just-for-fun I will
- ☐ draw a picture of my family
- ☐ glue a snapshot of my family here

"As for me and my household, we will serve the Lord."

Joshua 24:15

God knows where I live.
God lives with me.

I live at

_____

_____

_____

_____

_____

My phone
number is

_____

"God has said: 'I will live with them and walk among them.'"

2 Corinthians 6:16

Just-for-fun I will
- ☐ draw a picture of my house
- ☐ glue a snapshot of my house here

Rooms in my house

God watches me and takes care of me.

My house has _____ rooms.

My favorite room is

_____

I like it because

_____

_____

_____

Just-for-fun I will list ten things in my favorite room.

1 _____

2 _____

3 _____

4 _____

5 _____

6 _____

7 _____

8 _____

9 _____

10 _____

"I will lie down and sleep in peace, for you alone, O Lord, make me dwell in safety."

Psalm 4:8

The church is God's house.
I like to go to church.

The name of my church is

_____

_____

I can sing songs in church.

I can hear stories about God.

My favorite song to sing in church is

_____

Sometimes
I shake my
pastor's hand.

"I rejoiced with those who said to me, 'Let us go to the house of the Lord.'"

Psalm 122:1

My pastor's name is

_____

Just-for-fun I will sing "Jesus Loves Me."

♪ Jesus loves me! this I know,
For the Bible tells me so;
Little ones to Him belong;
They are weak, but He is strong.
♪ Yes, Jesus loves me!
The Bible tells me so.

I belong to God

God wants me to come to him.

☐ My parents brought me to God when I was little.

I was
    ☐ baptized ☐ dedicated

on _____

at _____

by _____

☐ I would like to be baptized someday.

"Let the little children come to me, . . . for the kingdom of God belongs to such as these."

Luke 18:16

Just-for-fun

I will draw a picture of me with Jesus.

Things I can do

God makes me able to do many things.

Just-for-fun I will check
the things I like to do.

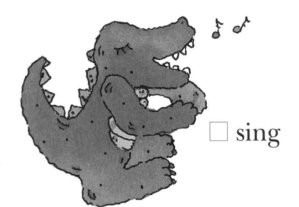

☐ sing

☐ ride
my bike

*"A happy heart
makes
the face
cheerful."*

Proverbs 15:13

☐ tiptoe

☐ laugh

☐ turn
somersaults

☐ eat pizza

☐ jump
rope

☐ brush
my teeth

☐ whistle

☐ run

God can count better than I can. He knows how many hairs are on my head and how many stars are in the sky.

I think there are _____ hairs on my head.

I think there are _____ stars in the sky.

"Even the very hairs of your head are all numbered."

Matthew 10:30

Just-for-fun I will count some things in my house.
I will write the number on the line.

__ beds

__ cats

__ Bibles

__ teddy bears

__ lamps

__ pillows

__ dogs

__ mirrors

__ chairs

I like colors

God made the colors.

I know my colors.
I will color the rainbow.

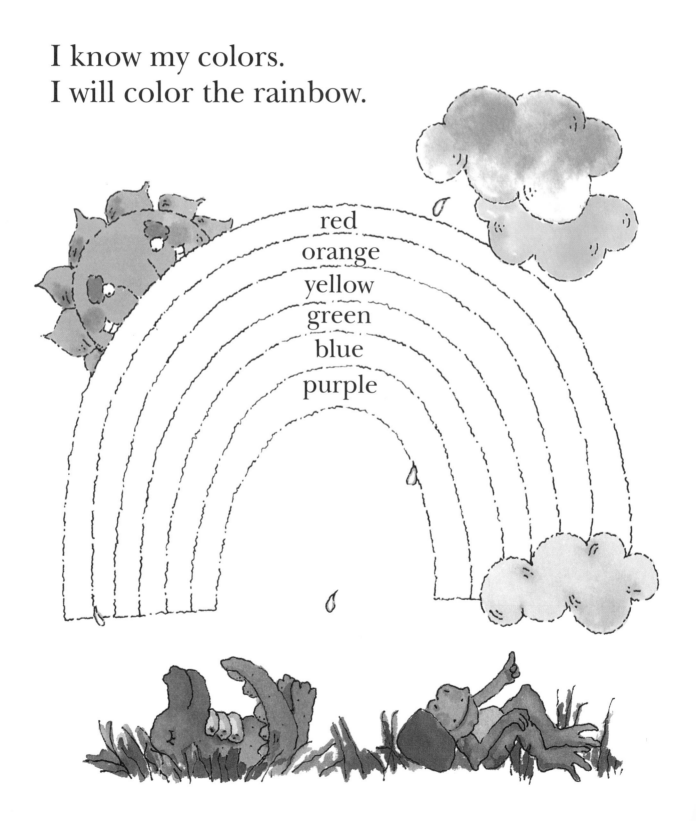

red
orange
yellow
green
blue
purple

My favorite color is _____

Just-for-fun
I will find five
things that are
my favorite color.

1 _____

2 _____

3 _____

4 _____

5 _____

"I have set my
rainbow
in the
clouds."

Genesis 9:13

I know my shapes

God makes things in many shapes.

In my house,

_____ is shaped like a circle.

_____ is shaped like a square.

_____ is shaped like a triangle.

_____ is shaped like a star.

Just-for-fun

I will draw a circle.
It is round.

I will draw a square.
It has four corners.

I will draw a triangle.
It has three corners.

I will draw a star.
It has five points.

"We saw his
star in the east
and have
come to
worship him."

Matthew 2:2

I like the seasons

God made four seasons.

They are _____, _____, _____, and _____.

Just-for-fun I will check what I like to do in warm weather.

☐ go swimming

☐ jump in puddles

☐ eat ice cream

☐ play ball

☐ pick flowers

Just-for-fun I will check
what I like to do in cold weather.

□ make
snowballs

□ sled

□ read books

□ bake
cookies

□ eat apples

"You made
both
summer
and winter."

□ build
snowmen

Psalm 74:17

I can see

God gave me eyes so I can see the beautiful world he made.

Just-for-fun I will use my eyes and find the ladybugs on this page.

"Come and see what God has done."

Psalm 66:5

I found _____ ladybugs.

I can hear

God gave me ears so I can hear
all kinds of sounds.

Just-for-fun I will check
the sounds I can make.

"Hear, O Israel: The Lord our God, the Lord is one."

Deuteronomy 6:4

I can touch

God gave me fingers so I can touch and feel many things.

Just-for-fun I will touch

something wet.
I touched _____

something dry.
I touched _____

something warm.
I touched _____

something cold.
I touched _____

"All who touched [Jesus] were healed."

Mark 6:56

something soft.
I touched

_____

something rough.
I touched _____

something smooth.
I touched _____

something fuzzy.
I touched _____

something itchy.
I touched _____

I can smell

God gave me a nose so I can smell
things I like and things I don't.

Just-for-fun I will tell you
things I like to smell and
things I don't like to smell.

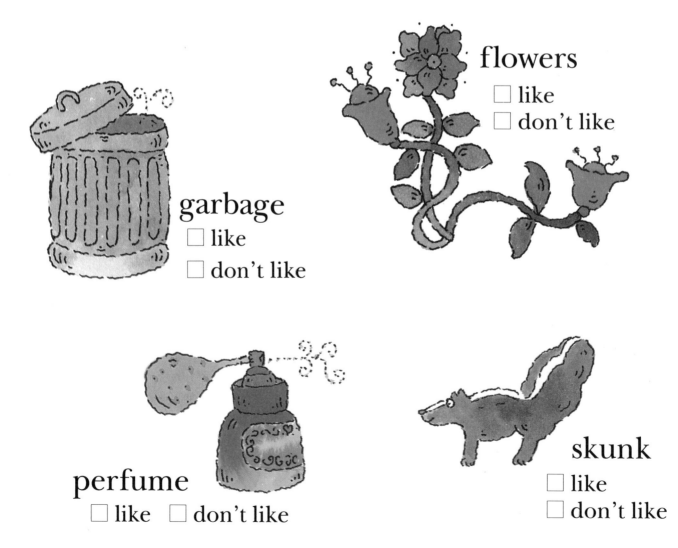

flowers
☐ like
☐ don't like

garbage
☐ like
☐ don't like

perfume
☐ like ☐ don't like

skunk
☐ like
☐ don't like

dirty socks

☐ like ☐ don't like

pine trees

☐ like ☐ don't like

popcorn

☐ like
☐ don't like

"Perfume and incense bring joy to the heart."

Proverbs 27:9

wet dog

☐ like ☐ don't like

When I smell something I like I say,

_____

When I smell something I don't like I say,

_____

God gave me a tongue so I can taste my food.

Just-for-fun I will circle the things I like to taste.

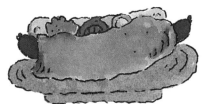

"How sweet are your words to my taste, sweeter than honey to my mouth!"

Psalm 119:103

I can feel

God gave me feelings.

Just-for-fun I will talk about my feelings.

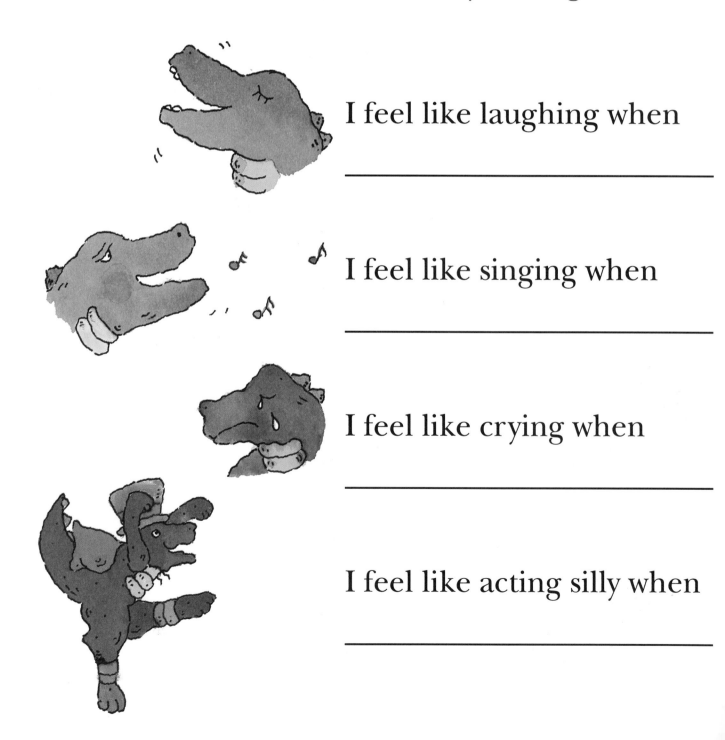

I feel like laughing when

_____

I feel like singing when

_____

I feel like crying when

_____

I feel like acting silly when

_____

I feel angry when

_____

I feel lonely when

_____

I feel like shouting when

_____

I feel scared when

_____

"There is a time for everything… a time to weep and a time to laugh."

Ecclesiastes 3:1, 4

I feel like praising God when

_____

_____

_____

God knows all about me.
I can talk to him in prayer.

I can praise God.
This is my praise prayer.

Dear God, you are wonderful.
You know all about me. I love you very much.

I can tell God I'm sorry.
This is my I'm-sorry prayer.

Dear God, I did something wrong, and I'm sorry.
I know it made you sad. Please forgive me.

I can ask God to help me.
This is my please-help-me prayer.

Dear God, please help me to be good today. Help
me to obey my parents and play nicely with other
children. Help me to remember to talk to you in
prayer each day.

I can thank God.
This is my thank-you prayer.

Dear God, thank you for my family and my friends, my home and my church, my clothes and my pets, my toys and my books. Thank you for making all things.

I can tell God whatever I'm thinking.

This is my prayer today:

Dear God,

_____

_____

_____

_____

_____

_____

In Jesus' name, Amen

Parents! This book is for you and your child to make together. Have fun learning Bible verses, doing "just-for-fun" activities, and making a record that you and your child will treasure forever.

Text © 1992 by Rebecca A. Egbert
Illustrations © 1992 by Nancy Woodman
All rights reserved
Scripture quotations are from the *Holy Bible,* New International Version.
Copyright © 1973, 1978, 1984 International Bible Society.
Used by permission of Zondervan Publishing House.
ISBN 0-8423-0502-5
Printed in Mexico.

99 98 97 96 95 94 93 92
9 8 7 6 5 4 3 2 1